The Complete Guide
For
Starting
A Small Lawn Care
Business

Written By:

Robbie Newport

The Complete Guide for Starting a Small Lawn Care Business

Robbie Newport

Published by Robbie Newport, 2014.

While every precaution has been taken in the preparation of this book, the publisher assumes no responsibility for errors or omissions, or for damages resulting from the use of the information contained herein.

THE COMPLETE GUIDE FOR STARTING A SMALL LAWN CARE BUSINESS

First edition. September 29, 2014.

Written by Robbie Newport.

Table of Contents

To Harold dog, my late co-worker and beloved friend.

Introduction

Starting a small lawn care business is something I've done successfully on three different occasions. All-together, I've been working my lawn care businesses for four years, and currently I'm working the third business, which is in its second year.

All three of these businesses have been a one man show, with me as the owner and operator. They were (and are) small lawn care businesses, operating without even a trailer until recently. I used a Toyota Van for the second business. As of now, I have the best set-up so far, with an extended cab truck with sideboards and a trailer. I'll get into the specifics of the equipment later in the book.

I just wanted to introduce myself and tell you why I'm qualified to write this book. Even though I'm not an expert in gardening, landscaping, and botany. I can guide someone in starting a small lawn care business. There's more to it than most people think, in my effort to explain, I'll try to make the book easy to understand.

There are a few purposes for writing this book. First, I want to help people find a way to escape working for someone else who is usually asking too much and giving too little. Second, I want to create an easy-to-understand guide for starting a small lawn care business so people interested can understand what exactly it involves and how to be successful with it. By the end of reading this book, you should have a good idea of what it's going to take and if it is for you. If you decide owning and operating your own small lawn care business is the right fit then this guide will get you started smoothly.

Benefits of Working for Yourself

Honestly, lawn care and gardening aren't something I'm specifically passionate about. The main reasons why I do it are: I can work for myself, it's peaceful working with nature, and lawn maintenance doesn't legally require any licensing or insurance.

When you have the right equipment and have filled up your schedule, the daily job becomes meditatively routine. Personally, this gives me the opportunity to listen to radio shows/sermons on my portable devices. Some jobs are more challenging than others, and when just starting out you'll have to tackle some jobs that'll make you ask, *why don't I just get a "real job"?*

No worries, the benefits of working for yourself far outweigh the negatives when it comes to lawn care. This is how my mind works at least. Personally, I don't do well with the cookie cutter corporate templates. Having co-workers and a boss is usually the part of "real jobs" that give me the most trouble. When working for yourself, you get to set the schedule wanted, work with who you want, and work for who you want. The freedom and flexibility are the best aspects of working for yourself.

However, there are down sides to working for yourself and doing lawn care as well. One of these is your income varies, as it fluctuates from week to week. Another downside for lawn care is it's a seasonal job, so depending on where you live this may mean a few months to half the year is mostly dormant. I will offer some remedies for the seasonal problem, but the non-guarantee of a fixed income simply must be accepted. Although, a close estimation can be made, especially after you get into a routine in the middle of the season and can average former months.

Working for yourself with a lawn care business is great in my opinion. I sometimes have to remember the many crap jobs I've had (at times mind numbingly idiotic) in order to remember just how good I have it working for myself. I drive my old work truck around on nice sunny days with my dog Harold and get paid cash, or checks, in my pocket after each day's work. Usually, I work jobs that take 1-3 hours, and I get paid nearly twice what I would working for someone else.

These are some of the benefits of working for yourself. Of course, there are many ways to make money working for yourself. Mostly, people are trying to work online or from home when thinking of working for themselves, which can be great. Having a lawn care business is different because you get out in the community and nature and physically exert yourself. This brings a different level of satisfaction than making money the easy way sitting in a chair. For those of you who are interested in doing lawn care, you know what I mean.

Type of Work You'll be Doing

T his might seem simple enough, but I want to touch on the type of work you'll be doing. This will weed out the faint of heart who think lawn care is an easy job. Although it isn't always that hard, there are times it'll test you physically to the point of wishing you had a pizza delivery job instead, so to speak.

When first starting your business, basically, you'll take whatever job that comes along, as long as the person offering the work is honest and it's conceivably within your capabilities. This often means you'll find yourself working unforeseen jobs in interesting situations. This is part of the adventure and fun of working for yourself. This is called paying your dues, but don't worry, because after a while you'll be able to selectively choose the preferred clients and weed out the less desirable ones. After a few months of building up your business, you'll have a solid group of clients you're happy to work for and will know generally what you're getting into from job to job.

Let me just throw some examples out there of the type of work I found myself doing over the years. Roofing repair, wood stacking, blackberry removal, fence building, digging holes, basic sprinkler installation, sprinkler pipe repair, painting, moss removal from roof, power-washing, gutter cleaning, window cleaning, lawn mowing, weed eating, aerating, trimming, hedging, organizing sheds, limbing, planting flowers, bark and dirt spreading and hauling, rock and sand spreading and hauling, garbage hauling, metal removal, and counseling. OK, so the last one isn't something I got paid for nominally, but it is something that generally happens as part of the job. See, your clients are usually older people who can no longer do the job themselves; from my experience, working for younger people is not as reliable or enjoyable. Anyway, you'll end up counseling or being counseled, if so inclined as a communicator.

This is a list of things I can remember doing, but it only tells half the story really. Being self-employed means you have to plan out the work and execute the job without someone telling you how to do it. Being systematic and thinking over the project you have, will ensure the job gets done in a timely manner in a way that satisfies the customer.

If you decide to start a small lawn care business, one of the main parts of your job will simply be trimming, i.e. weed whacking. This sounds easy enough, but from my experience it is generally the hardest aspect to your job. Trimming is the part of lawn care the average person doesn't want to do, this is for a few reasons. First when trimming, debris flies everywhere and it isn't pleasant being hit in the face with a rock or wet juices from torn up weeds you're destroying. People can't very well put on their flip flops and go weed whacking without finding out really quick, this isn't very fun. Second, people don't want to re-string the trimmer when it runs out of the string. This process with most trimmers has many old trimmers laid up in the sheds of America never to see the light of day again. Thirdly, trimming is simply an art that most people don't master. When driving around town, I see the average person out there with their cheap trimmers holding it like it's a rabid cat, they're tearing up their lawn in horrible ways, making a mess, and flicking rocks all over the neighbors' cars! I'll talk about trimming some more later, yet know that one of the major aspects that'll set you apart as a "professional" is having a good trimmer and knowing how to use it.

If you are just starting out and hungry to make some money, you'll probably be open to some of the odd things people have for you to do around their places. If you eventually get a power-washer, then you could find yourself cleaning up driveways, sidewalks, and even houses. As long as you're doing maintenance then a license isn't necessary, and if you are constructing something or landscaping then it has to be under around $600 to not be licensed. Check the regulations in your state for details.

The main point here when thinking about what the business will be like, is keeping in mind - it's not a cake walk. You'll be wrestling with nature and dealing with dangerous machinery. You have to be up for getting scratched, poked, gouged, have grass and debris go down your shirt, getting poison ivy, pulling spiders off you, having debris fly into your face and body from the trimmer, climbing up ladders to cut limbs and hedge, and lifting heavy barrels of debris and equipment. The pure physicality of the job is what I'm pointing out here, which can be strenuous.

Some other aspects of the job you need to keep in mind is the weather, customer service, and the business aspect. The weather is generally going to be sunny and hot most of the season, but this depends on where you live. At times, you'll find yourself working out in the rain and wind. The heat is the main factor in most parts of the country. Personally, I live in the Willamette Valley in Oregon and the seasons are fairly mild, but the in the summers the heat will get up in the mid-90's. Most of the summer is dry and hot, which for me tends to zap the energy out of me.

The customer service part of the job I'll get into more later in the book, but generally this is an important part of the job you have to be up for. Rather than the robotic corporate - appeal to the masses - type of customer service, you get to set the tone with how you want to deal with customers. My main advice is to be honest, clear, and consistent. Some customers won't like you no matter what you do, and others will think you are great even if you did just an average job.

The third part of owning and operating a lawn care business is the business aspect. The main thing to remember here is to be organized and have a system you can keep up with. Keeping track of all the details takes time, in addition to the work itself, and it's important to have a good system to make the job easier. I'll discuss this topic in-depth later as well.

Are you starting to get a sense of what it's like having your own small lawn care business now? Although mowing lawns is fairly simple, in order to have a working business that makes a decent amount of money consistently, you'll need to spend time thinking things through. That's what this guide is meant to help you accomplish, hopefully this has been a good start.

Equipment You'll Need

Starting a lawn care business can be relatively inexpensive, especially if you already have a vehicle that'll work. Having a truck is the best option, but you could use a van or even an SUV. I've even seen a guy using his bicycle with a trailer, so if there's a will there's a way. You might have to borrow some equipment from someone at first or get some used equipment to start. I don't know your situation, so this guide is going to be in general what I recommend.

Main Equipment:

The vehicle and trailer: optimally you want to have an extended cab truck that gets good gas mileage with some plywood sideboards. This truck will pull a small simple trailer. I use the trailer to put the equipment in, and the back of the truck to put the debris in. This makes the jobs day to day a whole lot easier, but for the better part of the first three years I had no trailer.

What you have to do, when you don't have a trailer, is put the debris in a tarp inside the truck bed and then wrap it up and put the equipment on top of it and around it. It's amazing how much debris you can wrap up and still fit your equipment in. If you have a large job with full loads of debris, you'll have to unload your equipment at the job and take the load to the dump. This isn't a garbage dump, but a debris dump in your city where you can also buy bark, dirt, wood, stones, and other forest products. Generally, these cost about $4-5 per load to dump. Get to know where these locations are in your local area, as you will be frequenting them often.

The lawn mower: this is going to be an important part of your business, so if you can - make sure to get a new one or at least one in very good shape. If you know how to fix equipment, then you can get an older one and keep it running, but if you're not mechanically inclined - get a new one. Having the right mower that runs well makes your days a lot easier, as inevitably you'll be cutting some challenging lawns. Make sure the mower is self-propelled and is a rear bagger. If you can, make sure it's at least a 6.75 HP engine and has big wheels on the back. I've had the small wheels most of the time, but this year I got the big wheels and it makes mowing that much easier.

The lawn care business I'm currently working is in its second year. The first year I got a used mower for $150. It was a Craftsman self-propelled, rear bagger, and had small wheels on back. It broke down right away which was worrisome, but with the help of YouTube I learned how to work on the carburetors and was able to fix it. It ended up working great all last year with only a few repairs. This year the mower's self-propelled cable went out in the beginning of the season. Instead of fixing it for use in the business again, I decided to invest in a new Craftsman mower. So, the mower I've used all this year has been a new one, which has made mowing easier and I don't have to worry about it breaking down. As long as I sharpen the blade every month or so, and tune it up every few months, it works great.

I've always used Craftsman mowers in my businesses, so I can attest that they're good machines overall. The top-of-the-line mowers are Honda, but they have been too expensive for me to buy. Any mowers you buy new are going to do well for at least the first year or two. You won't go wrong with Craftsman in my opinion for mowers.

Trimmer: getting the right trimmer is very important, as this is what's going to set you apart from the average person trying to do lawn care. I would recommend a straight shafted trimmer which you can turn sideways and create/maintain an edge in the lawns. Also, the straight shafted trimmer allows you to get underneath objects easier and puts the spinning head further away from your body.

When it comes to getting a trimmer, the best kind to get in my opinion is the SRM-225 Echo. This has an easy feed head, which allows you to merely line up the head with some arrows by spinning it around. Then you feed a precut piece of string through the hole in the head, pull the ends of the string on both sides of the head till they are even, then simply turn the head around and around until the string is wrapped up inside the head. This is an awesome feature that will save you lots of time and energy every time you have to re-string the trimmer.

Personally, I rarely use an edger and only recently purchased one. I simply use the trimmer to make an edge, but if you're going to do some high end or commercial type jobs then you'll want to get an edger eventually.

The string that goes into the trimmer comes in different thickness sizes. Getting the thickest size can really help in tearing down overgrown weeds and even blackberries. Generally, you'll want to use the medium thickness string. I would recommend using the Echo product string, as well as the Echo 2-stroke oil. Avoid the cheap 2-stroke oil, as it's not worth the money you'll save in the end when it comes to repairs.

Other brands that are very good are STIHL and Honda when it comes to trimmers and blowers. I'm not sure if either of these have the easy feed string feature though. These are also more expensive than the Echo, which costs around $200 for the SRM-225 model.

One more thing I'll say about the trimmer is depending on how much money you have and what kind of services you want to offer, you could upgrade to the $300 dollar Echo trimmer. This is the model you can remove the end and place other attachments onto it. For instance, you could get a chainsaw or hedger attachment to place on the end of the trimmer shaft. The attachments are going to cost you another couple hundred dollars, but the versatility you'll gain could be worthwhile if you plan to have more capabilities with your business. Obviously having these attachments will allow you to have much more reach and capability when trimming hedges and limbs that are hard to reach. Personally, I like to keep it simple and not offer the service of cutting high shrubs or limbs I can't reach with a smaller ladder.

Blower: cleaning up after you've made a mess is going to be the most noticeable part of the job to the customer. This is another part of lawn care the average person is lacking in greatly. When I drive by lawns that the average person has finished there's usually a mess all over the sidewalks, driveways, and porch areas. This part of lawn care isn't something people can do very well in flip flops while holding their ice teas.

So, getting a dependable blower is key to your business. There were times when I first started, I didn't have a blower at all. Thinking about it now, I don't see how I managed. I simply used a large broom to clean up afterwards, but if I saw the finished result now, I'd likely not be content with my work. You could get away with not having a blower at first, but I would highly recommend getting one. Having a good blower makes the job a lot easier and look a lot better.

Back-pack blowers are expensive, but they are usually the most powerful and useful models. STIHL is the top of the line when it comes to these. Almost always, I've made do with a Craftsman hand held blower, which does the job well enough. The business I have now I used an ECHO PB-251 at first. Echo is a great product you can't go wrong with in my opinion, and they aren't as expensive as the Honda or STIHL. I bought this blower used for $75 and it lasted almost two seasons. Just recently it stopped running and I haven't figured out why, so I had to scramble to get another blower. I found a used Homelite back-pack blower, which I've been using for the last part of this season. It doesn't run as well as the Echo and isn't even as powerful as the hand-held Echo, but it's getting the job done for now.

Misc. Equipment

Hedger: a hedger is going to be something you'll use every so often with certain customers who want their bushes and hedges trimmed back. Having a gas-powered hedger is optimal, because it gives you the ability to go where there's no electrical outlet and it makes the job easier. Yet, having a regular Black and Decker electric hedger with a long power cord will work just fine. I bought mine used for $20, but it was still in its original box unused. It's done very well, except I've cut open my power cord a few times. I had to splice my power cords back together and learn to be more careful.

Rakes: having a large plastic fan rake and a large metal flat rake are both going to be important. You can try to pick these up new or used, but make sure they're in decent shape because you'll be using them often, especially the plastic fan rake.

Large and small shovel: getting the large shovel with the short handle is absolutely necessary for almost every job you do. You'll be using this to scoop up the leaves and debris with the rake or broom. The small shovel is going to be used sometimes, but inevitably you'll find need for it. Getting both a spade and a flat head is optimal.

Broom: a large sweeper broom will be necessary for you to clean up the piles you blow together during clean up (sidewalk, paved street, etc.). Make sure this has thick bristles that aren't too soft or hard. This piece of equipment will wear out quickly if you're working full-time, so get this one new. Also, you might want to get a small hand broom to clean the back of your vehicle when unloading the debris.

Tarp: having a large 12' by 14' or bigger tarp is going to be important, especially if you don't have a trailer. Personally, I always spread out the tarp in the truck bed before I place in any debris and when I haul any dirt, bark, rocks, or sand. This way, when I'm unloading the product, I can grab hold of the edges and pull the remains out and have a relatively clean truck bed. Also, tarps can be used to spread on the ground to catch debris you're cutting or dropping from above; also, they can be used to cover equipment and other things when it's raining.

Buckets: having at least one large garbage sized bucket (est. 32g) is necessary for everyday lawn care work. Also, having small 5-gallon buckets are needed at times. It's best to have a large round bucket that has handles on top and also some indentions on the bottom for grabbing and dumping. Getting a quality bucket is important, as they endure a lot of wear and use. The bottoms of mine are the first part to wear out, because I drag them around with heavy loads on all types of surfaces. This large bucket is going to be what you stuff debris in every day, and then drag it over and dump into the truck. You might be surprised how much debris you can stuff into a bucket when you compress it by stomping on it. Having a couple of these buckets is a good idea, so when you're working a large project you'll make less trips to the truck. Lifting full buckets to dump them is one of the most physically demanding aspects of lawn care.

Small buckets are useful when doing detailed work in garden beds or transferring small amount of dirt to places. They also help in carrying tools or your sprayer around. These are inexpensive and useful.

Sprayer: getting a small (1-2 gallon) pump action sprayer is important and will be used often. You can get some Round Up type of weed and grass killer concentrate and mix it with water and then spray the weeds in the driveway and elsewhere the customer wants them gone. Make sure to get the customers consent when spraying and tell them to not let pets in that spot for a couple days. The sprayer I bought a couple years ago was $10 new and it still works and gets the job done. Backpack sprayers are optimal if doing large jobs, but this depends on the services you want to offer. By the way, a good rule of green thumb, use chemicals sparingly and only when natural remedies arc inadequate.

Gas cans: you are going to need at least two gas cans to keep the mixed gas and the non-mixed gas. I would recommend getting 5-gallon cans as it allows you to refill them less often. The mixed can is going to have your gas and oil mix for the blower and weed eater, which is generally 26:1 or 32:1, meaning 2.6 ounces per gallon or 3.2 ounces per gallon, respectively. The non-mixed gas is for the mower and power washer. Here is an important tip – use clear gas without methane, this gas is not available at every gas station, so find the stations it's sold at and go there. Methane gas eats through the rubber in the carburetors and causes engine problems, especially if stored with it for long periods.

Pitchfork: this tool will help you at times to unload or load certain debris and aerate some smaller lawns.

Rain pants and jacket: I bought a Coleman rain jacket and pants mostly for when I power wash, but I've used the jacket many times when it starts to rain.

Gloves: getting a lighter workable pair of gloves you are comfortable with is important to protect your hands. I would also recommend a heavy-duty pair of gloves for blackberries, roses, and the like.

Clippers: small hand clippers are a very useful tool for lawn care, as well as larger two-handed clippers to cut small limbs and bushes with; also, the large two-handed scissor cutter is necessary for hedging and trimming bushes by hand.

Limb cutter extended pole with saw: having a way to cut smaller limbs from the ground or a small ladder gives you more capabilities; this tool is about 6 ft tall with the saw and extends to about 12 ft. It has a cord that when pulled pulls the blade in and cuts the limbs. The saw can be used for larger limbs if have the energy and time. A chainsaw is the next step in expanding service capabilities, but isn't totally necessary when starting out.

Ladder: having at least a 6ft step ladder will come in handy and be used here and there, but in order to get up on most roofs, an extension ladder is needed. These can be expensive and aren't completely necessary at first, but if you look around you could get one for $50. Personally, I was able to get a used Cosco ladder that can act as a step ladder and also extends out to an extension ladder. Although it's heavy, it has come in handy for getting on a roof to clean the gutters or cut some limbs. For smaller jobs, where I just need a lift, I have a two-step ladder that I can also place tools on.

Sideboards: having sideboards will greatly increase the amount of debris you're able to load into your truck. These can be made for under $50, if you simply get a piece of plywood and cut it in two length wise. Then get a couple 2"x 4" boards and screw them on the boards to reach down into the truck bed. What I use to hold them to the truck bed, are clamps placed on the 2"x 4" boards and the lip of the truck bed. This has worked for me with a little wedging and manipulating. You can also paint your name on the side boards and get free advertising as well.

Extension cords: having two extension cords should suffice for most hedging jobs, a 50ft and a 25 ft extension cord should work if you have an electric hedger.

Wheelbarrow: this will be needed to unload bark, dirt, and other product, and haul it to a certain location you can't back up to unload.

Other misc. equipment that you'll want to have: large garbage bags, 2 stroke oil, string for trimmer, hand or walk spreader, thatch rake, machete, trowel, three forked hand weeder, extension pole pruner/saw, socket set, pliers, crescent wrench, electrical tape, duct tape, protective head muffs, sunglasses big enough to deflect debris, work boots, tough pants, tough shirts, hat, and some carburetor cleaner.

For a basic start, this is a good list of what you'll need to start your lawn care business and be ready for almost every job that comes your way. Some of these items you can start without until you make enough money to get them, but generally this is the equipment I have and use as integral parts of my business. One more note here is having the right equipment makes the job a lot easier so you can work smarter instead of harder.

I'll also add that the startup cost of the current business I'm running was around $1,000, and over the years has went to over $2,000 with the trailer and extra power washing equipment I didn't include in this list. The first couple times I started the business without having to buy the vehicle and not having a trailer I spent more like around $500-$700. The lower amount was because I got the equipment used for a low amount.

If you have to buy a truck and the equipment, you can basically add another $1,000-$1,500 to the amount. And if you want to get a trailer, this can cost anywhere from $200-$1,000 basically. So, if you are starting out without a vehicle and wanted a trailer and the proper equipment, I would estimate you are looking at around $3500 total start-up expenses to have your own lawn care business. Just keep in mind, these items can be re-sold and you'll then have a working sustainable income for as long as you want to work the business.

Building Your Business

T he first thing you need when starting out is faith that it'll work. This sounds easy, but in reality it is the prime aspect that stops people from working for themselves. There's no real way to know how well it'll work out before you begin, unless you've done this before. By reading a guide like this one, it's my hope that you'll gain the faith and confidence needed to give this business a shot. A guide like this also will prepare you for what exactly you're getting into and how to approach this wisely.

In this section, you'll learn what it takes to get your business off the ground, and I'll share my experience in how this works. This will alleviate the doubts in your head that this is really a bad idea and is not going to work. Having the right perspective is going to get you through the hard times when you find yourself wishing you had a "real job". In my experience having many of these "real jobs", my small lawn care business has been the best job out of them all, and I've had many different kinds of jobs to choose from.

If you're motivated to never again work around a bunch of disagreeable co-workers and bosses for a job that pays you too little and asks for too much, then you're starting to have the hunger it takes to grow the faith you'll need. Maybe it's not as big of a gamble for some people who can lose the money and not be ruined, but if you're like me - it's all or nothing.

With that said, I want to assure you that if you prepare and follow this guide you'll start to build your business and make enough money to compare at least with a min. wage full time job. That's a low estimate, because more likely you'll be able to average around $15-25/hr. without taxes being taken out (of course we are supposed to file at the end of the year). Personally, I only work my small lawn care business around 25 hours a week, because I have other work I do from home.

Just to give you an idea of a low-level lawn maintenance guy out here working his business, I make generally around $1100-$1500/month working around 20-25/hrs. a week. This after expenses, just to give you an idea of what you can make. I'm sure there are many lawn care businesses out there making much more, even per hour, but I'm content with this amount. Personally, I don't target the rich people neighborhoods because I don't enjoy working for most of them. I generally work for older people who don't have a lot of money. These customers are nicer to me and appreciate me much more than the rich people do. I've had some rich customers and still have one or two, and they're generally the jobs I dread the most. Maybe you're different in this aspect, but that's how I work it.

With that said, you still have to take the plunge, buy the equipment, and start advertising. All the while hoping and praying you're going to get some work and this venture will work out. The aspect of working for yourself that stops many people is not knowing exactly how much they're going to make in the next week. The unknown nature of the business can be exciting as well if you are up for the adventure. If you're willing to answer every call and do almost every job that comes about, you'll find yourself in some adventurous places doing some odd jobs. This beats the heck out of some boring mind-numbing service job in my opinion. Remember, as long as you're working, then money is being brought in.

Step by Step Process to Get Your Business Afloat

First step is to commit to the decision to starting your small lawn care business. Read this guide, mull it over, and come to a place where you are committed to giving it a go. Once you have this commitment, your success is going to happen. The calls will start coming in and your business will grow. As long as you aren't absolutely mean to your customers, show up late, and do a bad job, then you will be successful.

Second step is to get the basic equipment you need to be ready to work when you get the calls. At this point, you're on call and ready to go work. This also requires you to have a pocket calendar schedule you should carry with you at all times. This schedule will be how you keep jobs organized and times straight. Also, having a little note pad for numbers, addresses, and note taking while talking to customers is needed. Keep that schedule calendar, note pad, and pen in your pocket with you, ready to write down information to do the job. Also, some other paperwork you'll need is a receipt book and a bigger notepad at home you can write down all your customers in and keep track of all your income and expenses. And although seemingly obvious, I'll say that you must have a cell phone as well.

Third step is to advertise your business. This is going to cost a little money to get started, but is necessary to get the ball rolling. I don't know where you're located, but generally this is the advice I'll give. Advertise in the service section in the major local newspaper for a month, which will cost you anywhere from $50-$200. Advertise on Craigslist for free in the service section, I never had much success with this as it tends to solicit younger people who are less sincere, yet it is free and can work. Advertise in the free newspapers in your local area, this costs maybe $15-$25/month. Advertise on community boards in the targeted areas you want to work with business cards or fliers.

Another thing you need to do is get some business cards, or at least create some rudimentary fliers. I would recommend using Vistaprint.com for business cards, as you can spend less than $10 and get 250 professional looking cards. Business cards are key for you to get and give out liberally to whoever wants them.

If you have one or more customers already, then give them some business cards and tell them you are looking for some customers. Give them to your family and friends as well and tell them you are looking for some customers. You'll find out that most of your customers are going to come from referrals after the initial bunch you gain from this advertising campaign.

From my experience, the best customers come from the newspapers. The older clients who still read the paper and look in there instead of the Internet are the most reliable and sincere customers I've found. The customers who found me on Craigslist and online through places like Yellow Pages, have been troublesome and less than desirable. The customers that I've retained long-term are mostly from the newspaper and referrals.

Another couple strategies to use if you are really hungry for work is to make some fliers and go door to door in targeted neighborhoods placing them on the doorknobs. Also, you could paint your telephone number and business name on your sideboards as well as get a magnet from Vistaprint with your businesses name and number on it and place it on the door of your vehicle.

Fourth Step is to wait for the calls and respond well to them. Make sure you have your voice mail set up with a message for your business, so you can catch the calls you might miss. At first you want to be attentive during businesses hours and answer every call. What I did when I first started was hooked up my earphones to my phone, so even if I was in the middle of working and making noise I could hear the phone ringing and answer it. This way, I was able to catch the calls and build my business while working the jobs I did have. I would suggest answering with your first name, which you should put in your ad, for instance at the end of your ad put: call (your name) at (your number).

I just want to add here, this first part of the business is a bit stressful and will test your nerves. Answering the phone and being attentive to random people's request is not easy, but if you simply stick to the basics you can hopefully get the job and have a client that'll last for years to come. Some of the customers you gain are going to be your customers as long as you're working your business. This means, that call you get randomly can end up making you thousands of dollars in the end. Of course, you'll have to work for it, but when you find a good customer that pays well, is consistent, and is grateful, then you've found a gem.

After the initial building up of your small lawn care business, you'll have to do very little if any advertising. Most of your new customers will come through referrals, and unless you are wanting to do this 40-60 hours a week you'll stop soliciting for new jobs all-together. Some customers move away, don't work out, or even die, so every once in awhile you'll want some new customers. Unless you want to add some employees and grow to be a large lawn care service, then you'll max out with your customers and not need new ones very often.

Here is some detailed advice for you when dealing with customers at first. There's a certain routine way I handle calls from new customers. I answer with my name and they'll respond with who they are, I'll ask them "how can I help you?", they'll tell me what they need. At this point I'll know what kind of job this is and what kind of customer this is going to be. You will need to grow some discernment here to figure out in this short period how you're going to answer them. Some people give away that they are either really cheap or very disagreeable. If you're not desperate for money, then tell them you're not interested somehow. It just depends on the call, but believe me you will get some strange calls.

If you decide this is a person you want to work for, after they get done rambling on, tell them you can help them out and ask for a time and place where you can give them a free bid. If they ask you what your prices are, tell them generally what you charge, but most likely you'll want to see the job first. Just to note here, some people expect more than others, so even if it's the same sized lawn as another customers you'll want to listen to what this person expects to be done before giving them a bid. I'll discuss the pricing more in the next chapter.

Write down the time and the address and make it clear to them when you are coming for the bid. Make sure you know the area you are working as well, by having a map and studying it. If it's in a location you don't want to work, then tell them right away you don't go that far out. At first when you start you'll be willing to work further out. When I first started, I was driving all over the place, but after awhile you concentrate your customers and weed out the ones who are too far out, unless they pay very well.

By keeping that schedule calendar on you and writing down every bid and job you have, you'll stay organized and on top of things. It's very important you show up on time! If you show up on time when you said, they are generally already willing to hire you and pay you well. If you can't make it then always call and let them know you have to reschedule.

These are simple tips that'll help you build your business and get you afloat. The only other thing I would suggest is starting this process at least by May in most parts of the country. If you live in a place where lawn care is all year round, then this isn't as important, but in places where it's a three-season business, it's important to start this process in a timely manner. Optimally, you'll have the most success if you start this process in the middle of March in most places. I started the current business I'm running in the middle of May, and it was successful, but you'll have more success starting earlier.

Let me finish this chapter relaying some personal experience with getting my small lawn care businesses afloat. The first business I had my dad helped me out with getting a couple customers he used to have when he did lawn care himself. This and starting in February with advertising helped me eventually build up around 15 solid customers by May/June. The second business I started was in a totally different city and I started basically from scratch. I did have a couple clients which I did side work for when I was a house painter. These couple of clients and some advertising eventually turned into 25 or so consistent clients by June. I became very selective and even turned some people away because I had all the work I wanted by June. The third time I started is the businesses I'm currently doing. I had a couple customers from side work when I worked in an RV park as a maintenance man. This and some advertising done in the middle of May, helped me get around 20 consistent clients by the beginning of July.

Basically, you put that ad in the newspaper's service section and every week you will get 1-5 calls. Out of these calls, you should gain enough jobs to start keeping you busy. People read the paper on the weekend mostly, so on or right after the weekend is when you'll get the calls. Half of these calls are going to be customers you can work for regularly simply mowing their lawns, the other half are not going to work or are going to be random customers.

See, there are two kinds of customers, the random and the regular customers. The random customers can be one-time jobs, or they'll call you randomly to either do some odd job or lawn care. The regular customers are the ones who want to schedule you on a certain day and time every week or every other week. The regular clients are the ones you want to build your business around. They usually will have some extra work for you to do here and there, depending on their lawns and need. The random customers are usually going to be people you work for with an hourly wage, while the regular customer you will work on a bid. By working on a bid you will make more money than hourly.

At first though, you want to accept the random and the regular customers because you need to make some money and pay back the money you spent getting started. It's better to make something than nothing. After awhile you can be more selective. I'll talk about pricing in the next chapter, but this is just an insight to how it will play out.

Hopefully this section has provided some helpful insight into how to get your small lawn care businesses afloat. The main point is to be ready for the calls when you advertise. The trickle of customers coming in for the first month will turn into enough to work full time within a month and a half.

Pricing and Tips for Maintaining Business

T his guide isn't so much about the actual trade skill of lawn care as much as it is about starting your small lawn care business successfully. Personally, I'm not a gardener at all and hardly know a flower from a weed, so you don't have to be an expert in lawns or gardening. You do have to be a hard worker who pays attention to detail and is willing to learn. In this section I want to fill you in on how to set your pricing and also some important practical tips into the trade itself. This will hopefully allow you to start out with enough knowledge to seem like you know what you're doing to the average customer who thinks you are a "professional".

Pricing

Knowing how much to charge can be one of the hardest parts of the business when starting out. It has taken me nearly three years to become comfortable with pricing in a way I feel is fair to the customer and myself. Understand, this is only my perspective and how you set your prices is going to be subjective according to your perspective. What I want to do is give you an idea of how to approach this part of the business, so you can then build and modify it as you see fit.

I talked with an old timer lawn care business owner one time who was interested in buying my second lawn care business and he asked me how much I made per hour. I kept track fairly well over the season and knew I was basically averaging $17/hr., so this is what I told him. He sort of scoffed at this and said he makes no less than $50/hr.! This always has stuck with me, as I still can't figure out how he was able to make so much per hour.

I just wanted to show you how much this can fluctuate from person to person. Maybe he was working for the rich folks or was more of an expert than I was. I'm sure it was both of those things as well as he was just more willing to ask for more. I have the tendency to underbid myself, and over the years I've had to remedy this problem because nothing is worse than finding out you're going to be working for $5/hr. because of the low price or bid you gave. I'll just say, some people (like me) had to learn the hard way concerning this.

With my first two lawn care businesses I charged $10/hr. for labor and my bids were more like $15/hr. This third lawn care business I started by charging $12/hr. for labor and around $17/hr. for bids. Now, I basically charge no less than $15/hr. labor, and $20/hr. for bids. I'm finally comfortable with the amount I charge and what I make (this time ranging from 2006 to 2015). One thing you don't want to do is resent the people you work for because you asked for too little money. About a quarter of my clients regularly tip me as well, so getting tips is common with this business.

Now, the art of bidding the lawn is what you're going to have to learn from experience. I want to try and give you a head start in estimating what you'll face generally. There are many factors to consider when bidding a lawn, and getting it right is very important, as it could be the price you're stuck with for years. Clients don't like the prices being raised, although some will be more understanding than others. If you get older people used to a price, they may find another lawn person if you raise it.

The good part about this process is most lawns are generally in the $20-$30 range. The lowest I will do a lawn for is $15/mow, and that's only if it's every week and not far to drive. Mostly, $20 is the lowest you want to charge.

The factors you must consider are: how far away is the job from home, does the yard have a lot of bushes and plants, does the customer expect you to weed and trim the flowers and bushes too, do they want you to take the debris, is the lawn flat and easy to get to or uneven and complicated, how big is the lawn, does the customer make it easy for you to get paid and leave you alone, and finally how often do they want you to do it? This is a general guide to bidding consistent customers. Random customers who want some work done once or randomly, you'll have to consider the clean-up overgrowth factor.

The initial clean-up of an overgrown or poorly maintained yard is going to be about $15-$20 higher the first time depending on the extent of it. I've learned the hard way how much longer clean-ups take when it's the first time you've done the job. The trimming of shaggy edges and extra loads gathered up for removal take a lot longer than you may imagine at first. After you have the lawn under control and tamed, the routine maintenance takes much less time. So, always charge more on the initial clean-up.

I estimate the bids according to me making $20/hr. after expenses, which means after I pay for the debris removal, gas, string for trimmer, and any spraying. So, if I come to a lawn that I can see will take me 2hrs with the time it takes to unload the debris at the dump, then I will charge about $45-$50 to pay for the load, spray, gas, and string for trimmer. When trimming a fence line, the string will break off very quickly and you will use four times as much as with open air trimming. Keep these things in mind when approaching a clean-up.

Most of the lawns you'll mow once every other week. This will mean the lawn will be that much longer and messy and you'll make less per month than if it were every week. Consider these factors when bidding. Some lawns will be in-between a $20 and a $25 bid, so if it is a weekly make it a $20 and if every other week make it $25.

I always try and give a bid when mowing a lawn, even if it's just a one-time clean-up. Bids will make you more money, and after all the expenses and drive time that $20/hr. really turns into about $15/hr. profit. If it's simply a labor job doing something other than mowing, then I'll charge $15/hr. For example, this can mean trimming hedges, weed-eating fields, stacking wood, delivering product, and so on. Make sure to charge for any expenses on top of the $15/hr., so if you are picking up some bark for someone charge them for the gas and the bark.

A good rule of thumb as well, is to try and never use someone else's equipment. Unless you trust them and absolutely can't use your own then avoid doing this. If the equipment breaks then you're going to look responsible. With that being said, if you are mowing a large lawn and the customer wants you to use their riding lawn mower, then charge the $15/hr. The type of jobs where the customer has a good amount of work and wants you to use their riding lawn mower are worth it, because in the end you're making a good amount. Avoid working per hour for people who have a smaller job for you. Just use your discernment here.

These are the basics when it comes to how I deal with the pricing. Like I said, this is subjective and you need to be comfortable with what you're making and still make it appealing to the customers. Personally, I find that if I charge too much the customers will expect too much and be more disagreeable. To avoid the hassle of having to do a perfect job, and my work be examined too closely, I charge less. I still do a good job, but I can also joke around with them that I really don't know much about gardening or plants. I do know how to maintain their lawns though.

Basic Knowledge About Lawns

In this section, I want to give you some basics when it comes to the actual taking care of the lawns themselves. I'm sure you know how to run a lawn mower over them, but it will benefit you to know how and when to add product and repair troubled lawns.

One thing you want to do when mowing is cut nice and straight lines. Every time you mow, you should mow in the opposite direction as well. This will look better and result in a healthier lawn. Remember the lawns are alive and will respond to simply consistently mowing it.

The fall and spring are when you're going to want to add product to the lawns and repair them. This may mean fertilizer, weed and feed, weed be gone, lime, gypsum, seed, moss killer, or whatever else. The summer is usually too dry and hot to reseed, but if the customer waters then you could add some fertilizer or weed and feed. Most of these products you'll add to the lawn are granules or come in a sack, but weed be gone is a liquid which you can screw on the end of a hose and spray across the lawn evenly. This is effective in killing the weeds but not the lawn. Make sure you get the product that says it kills weeds, but not the lawns!

Reseeding and repairing damaged lawns will be about the most complex task you will have to do. I would recommend reading this guide, but also watching some YouTube videos on this until you have a battle plan and can deal with the different situations.

You'll have to assess the lawn individually and come up with an appropriate strategy. If the lawn doesn't have many weeds, moss, or damages areas, then I would skip any weed and feed/weed be gone/ moss killer products and go straight to reseeding it.

The most effective way to reseed a lawn is to aerate it first, then you can add lime/gypsum, fertilizer, and then seed it. Cover the seed with some peat moss or some dirt in the bare spots. Then instruct the customer to water it lightly 3 to 5 times per day for a couple weeks.

Aerating the lawn is best done with a large expensive machine that pokes large holes in the lawn and takes plugs of lawn out. You can rent these machines or you can simply get a small hand pushed aerator. Aerating a lawn can also be done by simply poking holes in the lawn with a pitchfork. If it's a larger lawn you can get a hand aerator that has spiked wheels on it. Personally, I have one of these hand aerators, in which I put a brick on the top of for weight then push it around the yard. This has worked well for me on smaller lawns, but if the customer wants the large aerator it's up to you whether you want to rent it and deal with the heavy machine.

Aerating is not something you have to offer; most people don't ask for it and so you can get away with not doing it when you first start. You can still reseed, but it just won't be as effective. The holes that the aerator pokes in the lawn help the seeds find a home.

Along with aerating you can use a thatch rake to pull up all the thatch that collects under the surface of the grass. Thatch is basically dead debris that collects in the lawns and creates a barrier of absorption that steals the water away from the actual grasses' roots. For best results on a lawn aerating and thatching it is recommended, but if you're not ready to aerate, then thatching at least can get the lawn ready to reseed.

After you aerate and thatch the lawn you'll want to spread some lime or gypsum. These products affect the PH balance of the soil in the lawn. If the soil is too acidic, then lime is needed, if the soil is too alkaline, then gypsum is needed to balance the soil's chemistry. In the Northwest where I'm located, the soils are acidic in nature because of the environment. In the south of the US, the soils are alkaline by nature. You need to investigate this for the area you are in to find out whether the soil is naturally acidic or alkaline in your region. These products are natural minerals and cheap to buy in bulk.

The next thing you'll do is spread some fertilizer. Personally, I use a 16-16-16 blend that is made locally so formulated for the North West. The numbers symbolize nitrogen, phosphorus, and potassium always in that order. Look into this further if you want to find the right blend for your area and business depending on your preference.

After the fertilizer you can add the seed. The seed you use should be a blend that is made for the region you are in, unless the lawn you're working has a different kind of grass than most other lawns in the place you live. If it does have a particular type of grass rather than the naturally occurring grass in the region you live, the customer likely knows exactly what kind it is. If the customer just moved in and doesn't know what it is, but you can tell it's different than other grasses in the area then take a picture and try to figure it what it is before adding the wrong seed. In the North West of the US, where I'm at, the usual grass here is Ryegrass and Fescue. As long as the seed I'm adding has the majority of these seeds in it, I can get away with adding some Bermuda grass or some other non-regional grass seed in it. Take some time and study the different grass seeds and it will help you sound like you know what you're doing and maybe even know what you're doing in the end.

After you reseed the lawn, put some peat moss or dirt over the bare spots in the lawn. This will protect the seeds from birds, embed them further in the ground, and protect them from direct sun exposure.

The final thing to do is water the lawn and instruct the customer to water it regularly for the next week. This is a very important part of the process in order to see good results. Because you aren't likely going to be back for a week or even two, it's up to the customer to make sure to water the lawn a few times a day. When they water though, they can't drown the seed so they float away in the runoff. The best way to water is to just keep it wet, but not drown it, and water every time it starts to get dry. Depending on the area you're in, this will have to be approached differently. Where I'm at it rains very often in the Spring and Fall, so this naturally helps the process even if the customer drops the ball.

Reseeding should be done every year in order to help the lawn get healthy and be full. If the lawn has many weeds and moss, then you want to first do a weed and feed/moss treatment.

Weed and moss treatment for lawns: if you're going to add chemicals to the lawn, then you can't reseed for at least a month. I would wait a month and a half before reseeding. If a lawn is in really bad shape, then put weed and feed granules and weed be gone liquid spray on the lawn. If you thoroughly spread these products evenly over the lawn, in as soon as a week you'll see a major difference. If this is done early enough in the Spring, then you can also reseed before summer. If not, then you should wait until the Fall to reseed it. You could add some fertilizer to the lawn in the summer if the lawn gets some watering either naturally or by the customer.

There are similar products meant for killing the moss in lawns as well. The moss will turn black and disintegrate mostly, but you can thatch it out after it has turned black. Again, wait for a month and a half before reseeding when applying moss killer.

The Basic Process of Yard Work

The basic process of your day-to-day jobs are going to be very similar. Every lawn and situation is going to have its unique challenges, but in general you're going to be approaching every job with the same process.

The process can be summed up like this: trimming, blowing the debris out of the beds into the lawns, mowing, blowing the debris out in the driveways or roads, picking debris piles up, and finally going back and putting the finishing touches on the yard.

This is how I approach every job basically, whether it's a heavily overgrown yard or I've been maintaining it for years. When I get there, I pull the trimmer out and cut the edges and clean up the beds, then I take the blower and blow out the beds into the lawn so I can mow over the debris, then I mow the lawn, then I take the blower and clean up the sidewalks/porches/driveways making debris piles, then I pick up the debris piles with my rake or sweeper and big shovel, and finally I go back through the yard and do some final touches (clipping, picking up larger debris, put hoses back, etc.). For cleanup jobs with bushes, trees, and flowers, I'll first take the clippers and hedger around, clean up the big stuff and go into the usual routine starting with the trimmer.

Dealing with Customers

Although you choose who you work for, you're still working for your customers. Dealing with customers is going to be one of the hardest parts of working the business. The great part about being the business owner is you can choose who you want to work for. So, when the customer wants to complain for instance to your boss, well, you're that boss and can say whatever.

This section could be very extensive, but I'm just going to touch on a few things I think will help you in dealing with your customers. Mostly it's a matter of having the right perspective when it comes to working this business.

One of the great things about having my own lawn care business is I can lose customers or quit working for certain disagreeable people and my business will still be rolling along and working. It may take awhile to get another customer in that time slot, but ultimately it doesn't matter that much. The nature of this business is you will have 15-30 different customers, so none of them can make or break your business. This basically means you can never lose your job! As long as you are willing to keep plugging along and finding new customers your business can survive losing however many customers.

Personally, this is one of the greatest feelings this business gives me. Another aspect to this same benefit is my business is still there even if I drop the ball and don't work it very well for a time. There have been periods of time when I was sick of the business and lost handfuls of clients, but I was still able to rally later and get it going full speed again.

You're going to get many different types of customers personality wise. Instead of getting into the types of personalities, I just want to give you some general advice. Approach each one with honesty and consistency and only do the work you are comfortable with for the price you are content with.

Being able to discern which customers you want to work for may take some time to perfect. Inevitably you'll be working for some that are harder than others. If there are customers who are simply too disagreeable, then simply tell them your grievances and move on. Usually these are the cheap customers and it's a money issue. After awhile you'll being to detect the cheap and troublesome clients right away and avoid them. Just remember, you don't have to put up with anyone's abuse or garbage, this is your business!

Scheduling and Paperwork

Before I mentioned you need a pocket calendar, a pad and pen, receipt book, and a notebook at home. This calendar is going to be your guide from day to day. What I want to talk about here is how to schedule in a way that is most efficient.

You have to decide how many days in the week you want to work and how many hours in a day. Once you decide this, then it's simply a manner of scheduling the work in. The most profitable jobs are going to be the bid lawns which are done on a regular schedule, either once a week or once every other week. These scheduled bid lawns are going to be the foundation of your business and are the type of jobs you want to encourage. Basically, they'll be around the same time and the goal is to make them routine and smooth with the work and payment. Some customers will be there and want to talk some, others will just leave the money in a certain spot and you'll never see them. You'll have to be careful not to get caught up with the ones who want to talk with you too much.

These are often older people and inevitably there will be some customers that'll basically talk your ear off if you let them. This is why I said you are a counselor as well. Personally, I like to talk to my customer some, as my purpose in life is not just business. Nevertheless, I can't afford to talk for too long, so I have to set my boundaries with some customers.

The way I schedule is by having different days designated for different parts of the larger area I serve. This way I don't have to drive too far between jobs wasting time and gas. This helps me compact my jobs into a shorter time period and be more efficient. For me, there are three days in which I have scheduled bid lawns and two days that I have for random customers and extra work for regulars. Because most of the scheduled bid lawns are every other week, then each week is a little different. Still, for those three scheduled bid lawn days, I only go to a certain part of the area I live in. After the first month or two of the season you'll have a set schedule for the most part and be able to gage how much you'll make from week to week and how much work you'll have.

When you get home from work, you want to write down how much you make and from whom. Personally, I use a numbering system where I give each customer a number. I have a notebook where I put down all the customers I work for (whether regulars or random) and give them a number in relation to when they became a customer. Some customers will only be one-time jobs, but you never know if they may call back. Program their names into your phone with these numbers and some indication that they are your lawn care customers. Then you'll know who is calling.

At the end of each week I tally up how much I made, how much my expenses were, how many hours I worked, and how many jobs I worked. Then at the end of the month I tally the weeks up and have a good estimate of exactly what I made profit and per hour. Just to note here, not every work week is

7 days. Some weeks are 8 days because months are usually 30 or 31 days. So, when you're calculating how much you make each week, keep in mind that two or three weeks in any given month (except February) are going to be 8 day weeks.

These are just some basic tips here in scheduling and paperwork. You are going to have to perfect your own system that works for you. Being organized will help you save time, money, and will alleviate stress.

Knowing Your Limitations

Depending on your expertise and what you're willing to offer in terms of services, you need to know your limitations. Being challenged with a job is different from trying to tackle a job you simply aren't knowledgeable or prepared enough to do. It's perfectly fine to tell a customer you aren't able to do a certain job. I've learned this lesson the hard way, and anymore if it's a job that I simply don't have the equipment or the knowledge to do then I say no thanks.

Also, be honest about what you know when it comes to plants and lawns. Remember, you're a maintenance person not an expert landscaper or gardener. If you're knowledgeable then great, but don't think you have to fake it to make it when it comes to this type of work. Maybe it means you don't get that certain big job on the hill, but believe me you're better off working the jobs which you don't have to act like you know what you're doing. Most people are simply interested in having an honest, reliable person come and simply maintain their yard and keep it under control. I guess the point here is to be honest and know what you're willing to do or not do.

For instance, a customer came up to me when I was mowing her neighbor's lawn the other day and asked me to come over and look at a job she had. She showed me this 12ft tall shrub that she wanted cut down about halfway. The shrub was thick and the area was cramped. When I was first starting lawn care I would have taken the job and dreaded the day when I had to tackle this huge ordeal, but instead I skipped it all-together and said it was beyond what I was willing or able to do, but thanked her for considering me.

Knowing your limitations and being honest about what your able or willing to do is an important part of working smarter and not harder. This will cure burn-out and stress while making your job more enjoyable.

Staying Motivated

There have been times when I was sick of lawn care and was ready to find a "real job" again. I would look around and see again all the reasons why I started a lawn care business in the first place. In the end, there are just too many benefits of having my small lawn care business to go back to working for someone else. The flexibility and resiliency this job offers are just too valuable for me to go back to shackling myself to some "real job". The only benefit of a real job is the consistency of the pay and there is no off season.

Part of what keeps me motivated is knowing I have security with my business. Even if I lost 90% of my customers tomorrow, I would still be in business and able to recover. This type of security in "real jobs" is unheard of anymore. Working for someone else usually means your job security is solely dependent upon one person, which is your boss.

While I'm working I listen to my mp3 player. Mostly I work for myself, unless my wife is working with me, and it's great to turn on a radio show or sermon and just enjoy the outdoors while I work. Wearing the big ear muffs means I can hear the headphones no matter what kind of noise I make. I slip the cord under my shirt and when I'm not listening I tuck the ear buds in my shirt buttons. Listening to sermons and Christian radio shows from the Internet are great ways for me to stay motivated.

Another motivation this business gives is the money I make. Working only 20-25 hours a week I make as much as I would full-time working for $10/hr. (yet keep in mind having your own business is an on-call job almost all the time.)

Finally, what keeps me motivated is I like the work for the most part. Being outdoors, smelling the fresh cut grass, and physically exerting myself to some degree is rewarding. Also, it gives me joy knowing I'm doing an honest job that's needed, not some sleazy job that's making the world a more sinful and meaningless place.

Ideas for Off-Season Work

D epending on where you are, lawn care is a seasonal occupation. This may mean that you're out of work for 2-5 months in reality. Where I live in the Northwest, the off-season lasts basically from the middle of November to the middle of March. This has been one of the downsides of having the lawn care business, but it can be a positive if you have something to do in the off-season.

The reason it can be positive is because it prevents burn-out and gives you a chance to take a long enough break from lawn care to come back refreshed and motivated. As long as we can find some way of making it financially through the off-season then this is a positive aspect of having a lawn care business.

One way prepare for the off-season is to save a winter fund. This could be 5-10% of what you make every month. If you are making $2,000/month profit, then this means you save $100-$200/month. If you work 8 months out of 12, then this is $800-$1600 saved. That would mean for those four months off, you'd have $200-$400 a month to help. This amount could be more if you save more or make more, but you get the point. Maybe it won't pay all the bills, but it could help you stay afloat when adding it too some other work you get.

Window washing and power washing are a couple more ideas that could make you some money during this time. Although power washing isn't going to be possible in the worst of the winter, you could wash driveways and sidewalks

45

when there isn't ice and snow. The lawns may be dormant, but the weather may still allow some power-washing. This is also a tool you can have throughout the lawn season and gather some work with. Washing windows could be done in the off-season as well. Window washing equipment isn't very expensive, and people do need this service done. Inside and outside windows could be cleaned throughout most of the winter.

One of the problems I came to when thinking about what to do in the off-season is trying to find a temporary job I could quit when lawn care season started again. This can be a difficult problem for some us. Personally, I work on-line selling books and stuff through eBay and Amazon as well as writing on-line. This makes me enough money to get through the Winter and supplements my work throughout the lawn season. If you're so inclined for online work, then this is an option for off-season work.

Seasonal work around the holidays. Some work can be grabbed especially during Christmas. Jobs like a delivery driver for Fed-Ex, selling/delivering Christmas Trees, telephone customer service for department stores, Amazon warehouse centers, or hanging up Christmas lights for residential homes. These all could bring in some income during the off-season.

Personally, it was hard to bring myself to working for someone else even seasonally. If you're like this and the area you're in gets a lot of snow, then you could have a snow removal business in the Winter. Get a snow blower and maybe a plow for a four-wheeler or your truck, and this could be a profitable business in the off-season. The equipment would be expensive, but if you're in an area that gets a lot of snow, it would be a good investment and solution for your off-season.

Another solid idea is cutting firewood in the off season. Depending on the area you are in, this could be something you did most of the year and then sold the wood throughout the Winter. A good chainsaw would be helpful for your lawn care business too.

These are some ideas for getting through the off-season. Having an off-season can be a problem, but with the right approach we can make it a positive part of the business. Being able to take a break from lawn care is healthy for us mentally as long as we have a way to pay the bills. With the right amount of for-sight and preparation, the off-season can also be a profitable time of the year.

Overview

Hopefully, this has been a useful guide in helping you get started with your own small lawn care business. Whether you already are working your own or are trying to decide if it's something you want to do this guide is meant to give some advice on how to start and maintain a successful lawn care service. Being successful to me means maintaining a consistent income I'm content with relative to the amount of effort I put into the business.

You may want to make more and expand to greater levels of success, or you may want to work the business less. Either way, lawn care is a good opportunity for you to work for yourself doing honest work.

One of the things that keeps people from starting a lawn care business or continuing when tough times come is there seems to be so many other people doing it. Although my wife is supportive of me, when I started my third business she was skeptical because of all the other lawn care businesses out there. It seemed there were so many guys trying to do the same thing. It never swayed me because I knew from prior experience that there's plenty of work out there to be had.

See, think about how many lawns are out there in the area you live. Now, all you have to do is get about 15-30 customers to have a full-time income. When it comes down to it, it takes many people like us to work our small lawn care businesses to fill the large need of people wanting their lawns mowed. And truthfully, if you're a nice honest person who does a good job and charges an affordable amount then you're a rare find and will be very sought after by customers. Most likely, you'll have more business than you can handle before too long.

After awhile, you'll be able to maximize the money you make for the time you spend working until you are making twice as much or more than a "real job". Besides, even if we made the same amount as working for someone else it's better to work for yourself. So, keep it in perspective and remember how great it is to be your own boss.

Now, there are many people out there who are looking to get rich by doing nothing basically. The only way you can get rich by basically doing nothing is by being in some vain and worthless business which adds to the problems in the world. Having your own lawn care business is honest work that's useful to society. You are there to help people keep their properties orderly and looking nice. Many times, you're also there as a friend to lonely old people and can encourage them in their life. Having a small lawn care business is extra rewarding if you care about the customers you are working for. These customers may just end up being part of your life for years to come. Personally, as a Christian I use this opportunity to minister, evangelize, and edify the Word of God with customer who are responsive to this. If they aren't responsive to this, then I'm just friendly and do the job well.

I know this guide is a bit lengthy and cumbersome in areas, but if you took the time to read it you're going to be better prepared to start and maintain a successful small lawn care business. At least that's my hope, and also to help you find a way to escape the slave-like jobs out there that ask for too much and give too little. Blessings in your efforts.

Don't miss out!

Click the button below and you can sign up to receive emails whenever Robbie Newport publishes a new book. There's no charge and no obligation.

Sign Me Up!

https://books2read.com/r/B-A-KODN-UPIMB

BOOKS 2 READ

Connecting independent readers to independent writers.

About the Author

I'm a Protestant Christian married man from Oregon. I'm a blogger, eBook writer, small business owner, copywriter, golfer, and history buff.

Read more at Robbie Newport's site.